of

ASHES AND PERSIFLAGE

of ASHES AND PERSIFLAGE

Aneek Chatterjee

Hawakal
PUBLISHERS
CALCUTTA   NEW DELHI

CALCUTTA | NEW DELHI

HAWAKAL PUBLISHERS

33/1/2 K B Sarani, Mall Road, Calcutta 80
70-B/9 Amritpuri, East of Kailash, New Delhi 65

Email info@hawakal.com
Website www.hawakal.com

First edition November, 2020

Copyright © Aneek Chatterjee 2020

Cover art: Shutterstock
Cover design: Bitan Chakraborty

ISBN: 978-81-948538-3-1

Price: 350 INR | USD 10.99

In loving memory of my elder brother,
late *Ranajit Chatterjee,*
who taught me values of
education and literature.

Contents

Introduction

Happy to present to you my third poetry collection, titled *Of Ashes and Persiflage*. The poems in this collection have been penned during 2018 and early 2020. Many of these poems were first published in reputed literary journals in the U.S.A., U.K., South Africa, Mauritius, Singapore and India. These are unrhymed poems, composed in free verse. I always believe that time is the best judge for any work. It decides what is good or bad. However, a poet feels happy and inspired when readers love his or her work. The same applies to this volume of poetry as well. If readers accept it, I will feel inspired.

The year 2020 has been a tumultuous one. The outbreak of Corona virus since the beginning of 2020 has exposed human beings to severe dangers and challenges throughout the world. Normal human life has become impossible, due to the spread of Covid 19. We are all covered with visible masks now, and all major events in every walk of life have been cancelled, including the 2020 Summer Olympics. Further, eastern states of India, particularly West Bengal, were hit by a severe cyclone, *Amphan*, in May. These apocalypses were quite perturbing for any individual. A few poems in this collection were composed on these catastrophes.

Two earlier poetry collections of mine, *Seaside Myopia* and *Unborn Poems and Yellow Prison* (both from Cyberwit.net) received favorable responses from critics and readers. I heartily thank all critics, Godfrey Logan, wonderful poet and editor of *Chicago Record*, Gopal Lahiri, noted poet and reviewer and Sandipta Kanti Nag, academic and literary critic for their rave reviews of my earlier works. My gratitude to numerous readers, poets included, of these two poetry collections for their warm and encouraging responses. Such love for my poems provides me fodder to delve deep into the world of poetry. I also take this opportunity to sincerely thank Bitan Chakrabarty and Kiriti Sengupta of Hawakal, noted authors and knowledgeable publishers, for a great production. Without their hard work and dedication, this volume would not be what it looks like now. Finally, I thank my wife Sarbani and daughter Prerna, initial critics of my compositions, for encouraging me always. Above all, if readers accept *Of Ashes and Persiflage*, my journey as a humble practitioner of poetry would get a real fillip.

Aneek Chatterjee
12 August, 2020
Kolkata, India.

Acknowledgments

My gratitude to the editors of different literary journals for publishing the poems included in this collection: Mary-Jane Grandinetti of *Shot Glass Journal*, Vera Ignatowitsch of *Better Than Starbucks*, poet Fred of *Ann Arbor Review*, Adrian Flett & Silviu Craciunas of *Poesis*, Quaz Roodt of *Poetry Potion*, Angie Tibbs of *Dissident Voice*, Amit Parmessur of *The Pangolin Review*, Kiriti Sengupta of *Ethos Literary Journal*, Sunil Sharma of *Setu*, Glory Sasikala of *GloMag*, the Editors of *World Congress of Poetry Anthology*, the Editors of *New Asian Writing*, Mossarrap Hossain Khan of *Café Dissensus*, Mitali Chakravarty of *Borderless Journal*, Onkar Sharma of *Literary Yard*, Pranab Ghosh of *Existential Problems*, Siddharth Sehgal of *Indian Periodical*, Sreetanwi Chakraborty of *Tech Touch Talk*, and the Editor of *Kafe House*.

Dilapidated Wall

The train that slowly moved
past a dilapidated wall,
pink flowers, suddenly took
a reverse gear

A boy surreptitiously
crossed a big hole in an
ancient wall to fish from the
black, silent pond;
pink flowers watching with
surprised birds and ghosts

And in winter nights,
the dilapidated wall crumbled
several times to allow dacoits
with big primitive guns.
The boy shivered in fear
till the morning whistle
of the locomotive creates
a rhythm of safety
and silent laughter

This Afternoon is Grey

This afternoon is grey
Rains slashing the window pane
Dark clouds have nestled on the platform
Surreal humans move slowly
ignoring rains and clouds
White flowers begin to smile
perfectly against wise clouds

Me and train have been
dwelling in this station for
thousand years
I know every bit here,
rains, all humans and their movement,
mystery clouds
and brown doors ...

This afternoon is grey
All lights were switched on early
I know every bit of this
surreal world, brown door, every bit ...

But I never knew
I loved grey so much

Barren Page

I stitch words
for a ballad
& decorate these on my page

When I open the page
It's only a tabula rasa ...
Where are my chosen words?

Where is my favorite
ballad?
In utter disgust, I look up

The old ceiling laughs
with fugitive words; I command all
to jump to my page

In persiflage, the ceiling
vanishes into the blue
& I sit dark in a corner

For a Woodpecker

Make some holes in the bone
like the woodpecker
creates, to let some shine
in
She decorated herself
after twenty years of death
when this house
on circus avenue laughed.
All lights, glitter, guests,
food and drinks of a
wedding;
pretty flowers like the new bride
Lights gradually turned black
in a deserted circus
Face seemed like a dry
river bed full of
angry lines
& all windows to the edifice,
big & small, crumbled one
by one

Twenty years is a long time
Red buses turned blue & yellow

A new metro runs under the city

Now she takes a ride in the metro
that journeys into
the big double deck
red bus
Freedom calls for some
shine too
through tiny windows
in our bones & skin

Welcome woodpecker,
create those survival windows
Circus avenue has been renamed
recently

Home

When the tree shed all
leaves under a blue
naked sky,
someone whispered: it's spring

I sat a crow on the barren tree
that melted down before
the black bird escaped
in to oblivion.

Pebbles strewn around
the pathway laughed
& walked straight
into my heart

When I found the gate
locked after a long journey,
the road announced,
'you're home'

Coveted Seat

A sudden splurge of air
invaded me
My senses were numbed
& I metamorphosed into a big
balloon.
Leave it to you to imagine the
color, I could not figure out

As the day progressed I flew
to different locations, adorable spots
you worship, men & women living
in high altitude
I flew high, bigger, with dense energy

When evening descended on
earth, I decided to kiss my soil
But my (dense) energy
took me high, higher
& I found a great seat on the
mountain top, & I jumped
to its lap

But the naughty beast fled
from the spot
to a tree top
& I flew again
& I flew again from tree top
to tree top
But the coveted seat played
hide n seek, incessant

I'm still flying
I'm still flying in danger
without energy & color
you're unable to
figure out

Piece of wood

Mirror saw a lanky piece of wood
& whispered: still dream
green to flousrish ?

Dark fantasies reappeared
Black smoke laughed loud
& embraced lanky wood

The mirror survived,
but the piece of wood
broke down in shame

& the mirror stood alone,
as always.

Fossil

Visited the museum yesterday
In a dark and cold room came across
an object, crawling for some warmth

I could not utter 'hello, how are you'
But the poor creature, surprisingly alive,
saw me and smiled in agony

'I knew I would be here someday,
But I never knew it would be so early',
the creature said with difficulty

'you idiots made a hue and cry
over my health, fought over me,
but could not save me'

A fossil quickly retreated
from the sight of another,
demos kratos

Blue in Rains

Summer gone, rains
came
Dark clouds I always
loved, mystery embraced
trees and mountains,
my mind

Summer gone, rains
came
But the sky remained
blue
Your color a month ago
Mystery embraced my mind
as it turned blue since then,
in rains and winter

About time & pride

Sometimes I'm ahead
of time I yearn to be.

The magical night laughed at me
I was at the airport, & the next
flight to Nice was in the morning,
eleven hours later.
I didn't know how I beat time
when I slept on the floor,
with my cabin bag as pillow &
my left hand inside the strap,
as if it contained hundred
years' of accumulated wisdom.
I didn't know how I beat time
& possible cheaters.
A little drunk
& the night passed in a whimper,
aimed at transborder
lumpens.

In the morning, I found
my bag open, and some coins
& paper on the floor.

I picked up all & realized
these actually escaped
my powerful pocket.
I searched my toothbrush
& saw in the electronic board that
my dream had left for Nice.

Howled at the beginning &
then laughed, pitied me & time
lazily at the wash room,
always my best bunker;
& waited for the next flight
eight hours later.

I'm still ahead of my time,
yearned pride & dream

[Untitled]

Evening descended
on a platter crafted
out of bones
A little chill in the air
the last eagle was
hovering for her prey
Trees, naked, due to prolonged
treachery, was
guarding my father
He lost his voice
to a morbid evening
before he succumbed.
Two drops fell from his
eyes, invisible dew

I tried to collect dew on
the platter; but it slipped out
in the cold, his bones
in the tree

Dead Men

Dead men talk to me
sometimes, always
They have framed their smiles
Neither wide, nor short, measured
They have devised unique routes
of dialogue, uniquely monotonous

They look at me, but they look beyond
making me turn, only to sense their eyes on my
back
Bemused, I try to take my own route
But they are everywhere, eager to talk n see
Dead men, talk to me with a framed smile
sometimes, always

Skeleton

Standing alone in front,
of whom I don't know

It may be a river, a skeleton,
crab, mountain or window

Pensive at dusk, once a river
invited, but refused a swim

The skeleton laughed to see me
under flesh and skin, thick

This crab was supposed to walk on earth
But oxygen had a history of treachery

I see several windows in you
But unable to escape like a river

Inside the cottage

She looked at the hills
clouds settled there,
floating in the air her wish
her home

Clouds looked at her,
talking to the trees
for an abandoned
cottage where squirrels played

Squirrels looked at her,
wondering how small animals
feel happy with straws and leaves
in the open green

She comes back green to routine,
where clouds nestle in the hills
trees and squirrels are busy
playing inside the cottage

Chocolate Square

they won't allow me to the podium
so i climbed up a tree with great difficulty
i could have climbed the podium
with much ease; they won't allow

the tree is much above the podium
much higher to me, my now forgotten id,
much higher
the happy chairs look so small,
flowers decorating the podium look so plastic
faces of vibrant dead men are nothing
but surreal paintings and the lady announcer
vanished all of a sudden

the podium invited me, why, i do not know
they obstructed my entry, why, i do know
happy chairs turned sad, why, i don't know
plastic flowers appeared real, why, i do not know
why the lady vanished, i don't know
why I climbed up the tree, i do know

my solace, my id now scanned the podium
my tired hands and legs instructed me
to stay on the tree
chairs look so small, and the podium
a little box i fancied as chocolate square
in childhood
chocolate chairs adults prefer
in a little box

Ruins

Not easy to sleep
in ruins
the debris, the holocaust
come back in short naps,
if these are called dreams ...

Ghosts dancing with the wretched,
It's difficult to keep a tango

Chairs are running after men and women,
afraid of coming closer, always

This air is full of wry smile
and unending persiflage

How long can one survive insomnia?
Sleep has learnt to sleep in ruins, now

Game

The metal disc, shining & heavy
goes up, up in the air;
players below scuffle
to get it ...
all in dark.
It may hit a player,
(s)he may be injured,
but never within.

This is the rule of the game.
Spectators sit in the dark.
The playing field is dark.
Positions alter now and then
A spectator changes
in to a player any time,
and vice versa

Everybody is comfortable in dark,
everybody seems happy

A bleeding player retreats

A happy spectator takes his place
But the game continues
through the night.
Surviving players will resume
the game next evening,
only in the dark

Everybody is happy,
everybody is game with
the shining disc here,

in dark, cold evenings

Colors

Everything has a color
the color of desire, the color
of want, of love & hatred

Our journey has a color
Our motivation, betrayal,
vision & senses

The color I see gets colored
according to my desire, my wish
my ego, my people

Long back I preferred white
After I scribbled so many wants on white
All colors became unknown to me

Silhouette

Night is drifting away ...
Night is drifting away
like pensive liquid
in a red glass
A shrill voice
from another planet:
popular bolywood
And that silhouette
in between sand and sea
drifting away with white liquid
in a red glass, miles at night.

Shrill voice, bolywood, november,
popular band drifting away...

with pensive white.

Three Cheers for Lucy

Love blossoms only in
hoardings & banners here
hatred deep inside, sacrilege
Three cheers for Lucy
Long dead Lucy

Flower blooms only in
newspapers
Rocks & sand decorate
all gardens, greens
of earth, morbid earth

We only shout for love lost
Surrounding air absorbs
all yelling
& turns guilty

Grasshopper

Met the sky at the end of the
barren field, exactly where the line
was drawn forty years ago

It was bright orange, attractive
when I started, and a new alcoholic
yearned to touch the line

Suddenly darkness jumped on
earth like a grasshopper, and I
faced an endless vacuum

Spoof again
as reality drifted from
visuals I'd painted all along

Looked back to search the
starting point for some light.
Only the grasshopper smiled

In the Name of Pandemic

Locusts have lost their ways;
so have we
Trains have forgotten the rails
and the daily laborers.
So have we.
Humanity weeps in hospitals,
offices and bylanes
we don't visit.
Earthquakes occasionally provide
jolts we experience in
daily life
But the dinner table is
ecstatic with an extended leisure
Only the elephant desires to have
a chair under the chandelier

Mythology of Mind

When night was retreating for dawn,
someone pulled me up in dark ...
how are you my dear ?

I wasn't in my senses
and longed for
a glass of water

He gave me water,
and slowly uttered,
how are you friend ?

A deep trance murmured,
I'm not well; words
divorced me treacherous

He smiled, and the long whistle
of a gasping steam engine reached
rooftop in a silver night

Three children waiting

in the moon for an elder sibling
from the borders

That 'someone' yawned, and five dogs
stopped barking and began
waiving tails in a summer night

A ghost from the mythology
of mind started pulling a long chain
in awed whisper

And I was writing again
as dew drops found estranged
lyric in an autumn morning

This Summer

Every summer brings back
an obnoxious ghost
who sat in different branches
of the mango tree
& made these swing
A few urchins only saw green
mangoes swinging
in front of their eyes
They threw stones at the tree
to have a taste of green fruits,
but in vain.
Hence, the ghost laughed

Every summer the nagging scent
of the jackfruit came with father
making little minds shake like
the proverbial earthquake

Every summer, donno how,
vocabularies got strengthened.
& in one April morning,
sex came to an eight year old
sending a chilling ecstasy down
his spine

Summers are different now.
This summer my vocabulary
said hydroxychloroquine.

& you know,
the obnoxious ghost
laughed again

Green Packets

When i try to touch
the lump
in my throat, projected
fame telephones from
the TV screen
&
the weather comes as
huge confusion.
Every night I think of delving
deep in my freedom, poetry...
peace, solace,
twisting eyebrows & also,
a slice of this weather.
As morning beckons,
I venture out
for the university,
with two green packets, —
hope in one, and despair
in another
A student dribbles his hand
through standing men
in the queue
to touch my feet

& i die of shame
& confusion
& when i try to touch the lump
in my throat, projected
fame telephones again from
the TV screen.

This night I'll try to
steer out
of the weather,
but, afraid,
face it again tomorrow,
day after, or
in the queue

Of Ashes and Persiflage

The iron curtain separates death
on both sides, separates the corpse
and ashes and fire.

Life watches from the eastern side
of the iron rail, with the dead body,
waiting to be pushed to the
pyre on the west.

The corpse' waiting to have
a date with ashes, after some
heated time with fire.

Relatives wait, and friends,
and sons and daughters,
sisters and brothers.
Melancholy waits, and silent tear.

Chair looks at the corpse
for one last time, and status.
Belongings, wealth and
ego watch in persiflage.

The fire is waiting,
time is waiting, and the ultimate ash,
to embrace all hankers, ladder, perfume
and vanity; you and me.

The Music

A day to adore is often
a day lost
The coconut juice someone
says water, spills over
& the wet patch banters
in persiflage
Sunshine galore, humans move
in haste, slowly
Bodies chasing bodies
day after day

The music goes on with
guitar, drums, saxophone,
without any tune I search
to treasure

April Evening

From my terrace in one April evening
I watched the full moon, but it
looked pale pink

& suddenly melancholy gripped me
Where was the gold ?

& I saw policemen announcing
measures to combat Covid 19

The cool breeze that flows
during this time, eloped with a black crow

I came down & jumped to my bed,
my only escape, & fell asleep.

Suddenly a golden aroma covered me
& I saw my favorite platter smiling
through the rectangle, in an April evening

Flashes from the Pavement

When rain comes, don't know
why, you also come
Not like rains, but like dark clouds
covering every bit of my sky.
& occasional flashes bring back
to me tales from the pavement,
small alleys, riverside, busy streets
and an indifferent boulevard.
& when rains pour incessantly,
I get drenched in
sweet & bitter coffee
& laughter, cries & disagreements.

When the sun reappears, you hide
in me, to be bloomed again in
a rainy day.

Sunset

West I treaded
to see the desired,
but watched only a sunset

Walked north to find
home, but discovered
the melting glacier

East I embraced
for glittering bright;
a storm swept me off

The hapless creature now paints
bright glacier on dinner table...
in the dark

Bodyless Wanderer

The aroma is attractive, draws
everyone close, like a magnet
hooks ordinary
iron pieces.
Power is important
in (vocabulary of) politics,
& society too.
How powerful is powerful
& how powerless is powerless,
no discourse on politics or society
could ever decipher.
It's a bodyless wanderer which
seeks shelter in the entity
of a person
or group, like a mystic spirit.
It rewards our ego, id, lust
& desire
It nurtures us healthy,
for the ultimate fodder

Because the bodyless wanderer
finally crushes the beholder,
after crushing everything
for him, her

Corona

Show your stockpile
of weapons of mass destruction
to corona,
it will laugh silently
Show your sophisticated war planes
and submarines, it will
mock
Show your 50, 60, 100 floor
skyscrapers, it will fly
there

& from the top,
advice you,
humans,
think fresh, think anew
There was
something wrong with your
ideas

Narrow Window

A slice of sky
is bisected with the electric
wire from
my bed
A tiny bird visits and
sits on the wire, daily
Talks to the sky and measures
me; I try to talk
But it ignores, and looks up
to the sky, stoic

Leaving ashamed my
narrow window, bed,
id

Ephemeral

We met again, suddenly.
The script was ready
We talked about local
& national politics, & agreed
that it was a blank phase
We discussed possible solutions,
but the noise in the fair
could not provide any

I tried to talk poetry
& he said, let's meet sometimes
and chat for a long time;
& I agreed...
Thrice in the last four years

We departed soon, without
fixing any time & place for our
long chat...
Thrice in four years.

Resurrection

Some issues are so puzzling...

Often I ask myself, where does
mind stay...
In the brain, heart or eyes
or in thin layer of the skin
when a touch ignites
irresistible passion

& I get more confused...

When I look up, clouds
paint me words, images,
I lost in a forest of bricks
of dingy bylanes;
in the asphalt of avenues,
smell of markets.
Clouds, white, black or sepia
hold me inside, and I float...

I float and finally
descend down on
the skin of narrow bylanes
& avenues;
in the heart of the city center,
& discover me there

Fresh as ever

Afternoon

The April afternoon melted
like sugar cubes in our coffee cups

A new color has adorned the sky;
difficult to paint in memorabilia

Thought we essayed color
to the coffee table;

sugar cubes only mocked us
from the drowsy pot this afternoon

Beggar

It heard whatever you said
in silence
Look, just a single white rose
bloomed in the garden
after so many years
sensing your
presence
I heard there would be a
lunar eclipse tomorrow
But my ocean had already
started surging
Look there is no beggar on
the street today,
except one waiting for
another quake

The white rose is also
waiting in silence, after
so many years

Evening

Melancholy grips this
winter evening
An indifferent city has not
come back home
Buses, trams & taxis jostle with
hand pulled rickshaws &
individuals for a little space
A lonely crow shouts from
an electric wire to make way
for the ambulance stuck in a
terrible melee

& the patient inside
painfully watches fading
light of the winter evening

Lizards all over

Lizards crawled over my body,
stone wall,
could not dispense with

Lizards all over, fat, thin,
tall, short, jovial, serious
Prying eyes, dark tongue

only watched helpless.
But mind threw them all
to the woods, slushy water-body

Lizards all over
crawling on a supportive
stone wall, with colorful flowers

Pavement

Boiling rice was talking
to the pavement, angry
A broken piece of mirror
looked at the tattered clothes
& the adjacent tree,
naked, non-appointed guard

Buses waited for a while, but
left hurriedly for their
destinations
A lady sprayed irresistible
aroma, went away

I left my nascent poem
orphan, like the child waiting
for boiling rice

Agony

Every time I try to enter,
the door is
indifferent

Every time I try to exit,
the door is
different

Dark

Poetry in dark times,
you seemed to be; or
so I thought

There was no beacon
of light, no word to blow me
off, no syllable excellent

The meaning of dark is different
to different souls; my skeleton
dances in the lighted floor, only in dark

Dark nurtures innovative skills
only the shining knife knows, as
well as shining minds

Let me grow in dark, eternally.
My skeleton is far away from
dazzle, & startling words

Red Rose in the Courtyard

I know a man
who takes a red patch on
his shirt as a leaf of rose.
The man wants to
plant a tree of rose in
every heart, without thorns.
He wants us to believe that
everybody's speaking his
or her mind, and
could be trusted all along.
The man laughs loud,
incredibly loud,
but never cries; because
he thinks that his pain will
pain others.

Remember the last storm?
Actually it was a tornado
that devastated everything
around
I searched for the man
after the storm, and after
huge efforts,
I found a red rose in
his courtyard, laughing
loud at me.

Stained Blood

Dear flower kept between
pages seventeen and eighteen
smiled after forgotten years.
Stained blood reminded of
a fading park, roses, blurred
rains, and two strange birds.
Winter turned spring only last week.
Roses, white, yellow and red
bloomed inside.

But page eighteenth got dried,
stained blood I had never forgotten

Hide & Seek

I play hide & seek
with you, myself.
Sometimes
I do murmur lost songs, favorite
poems, surreal images

& when I wake up
& land in my swanky office,
a surreal painting adorns
the wooden wall
I've kept a few books of poem
in the rack to woo the visitor

Now I start playing
hide & seek
with you, music, poetry
& me

Mask

Flowing river
let everybody know
I'm not well.
My vanity, my id could not be
washed in pristine water ...
Each day spells gloom of a
mind in black hole,
captivated for million years
& the day is without odour
or light

The river returned on
a full moon night & informed
ashes covered every valley,
rendering the
body & mind muddy

& I murmured: let's wait for another
big bang to wash my mask, id

Without Burning Wyes

hear me in silence if you like
as i unfold for the first time
the sparrows are talking again
on the cornice this morning
as always, rubbish, take me away

waiting for the yellow flowers
that last bloomed in december
three years ago, in december three
years ago, i can vividly remember
three years of abortive attempts
look at the eyes of the tiger, still burning
late king killed it fifty years back, but it's
standing like a valiant tiger,
dead but burning

the small lake is full of water lily, and
bushes surrounding the lake have grown dark
and deep where we kissed for the first time
when the king killed the tiger, and the plane
flew to the US five years later, to new jersey
to be precise, & green envelopes turned
sophisticated yellow gradually

& the king also killed you, but you're
reborn in a distant land, & he killed me
but didn't decorate like a tiger
i was animal without burning eyes,
waiting for yellow flowers to appear

sparrows also talked on the cornice
that day, rubbish, take me away

Diary of the Skeptic

When i shout peace
autumn leaves
remind me of a blood bath
in a remote hamlet
& i see red in every
tree, clay barren road,
every sky

When i say justice,
my raped sister laughs
inside the mirror, she used
to look decent

When i utter noble words
my image in deep, dark water
breaks into several
ephemeral rounds
& mocks me

Ignorant

I know everybody here ...
The gentleman with brushed
hair and neat trousers, blue,
white & black shirts.
The beggar on the street
& wonder how he's fixed
in his place every day.
A group of boisterous school boys,
jumping & fighting their
way back.
The lady with a big sunglass,
& changing hairstyles.
I know the old tree, & the
tea shop beneath, where the local
leader, with his men,
sells dreams.

I know everything here ...
Potholes on road, pale
dustbins, and smashed papers
where disgruntled poems
wished to make a
permanent shelter.

An unfinished building,
where a group of men
play cards in the afternoon.

I know every lane & bylane
here, which get submerged
during rains, and dark after
evenings
& the small tree that
produces white flowers
day after day

But I have never come to know
white flowers &
disgruntled poems;
agony of potholes & the
spectre of dreams the
leader constructs so carefully,
every day.

Inside Out
(A Poem dedicated to Kolkata)

Wrinkles on my face
are like unhappy lines of
a dry river bed.
They're saying
I'm getting old. In every winter
breathing trouble ails me
& I'm unable to express my feelings
due to intermittent bouts of cough

Arteries & veins inside my body
are getting thicker due to trashes
gathered from society & flow of
oxygen to my heart is getting choked
day by day

But believe me, I'm young at heart
I still love migratory birds to adorn my gardens
I like mothers peeling oranges for their
children in sunny winter mornings
I like the tingling sounds of
uncertain trams sailing over
I play football with both

green-maroon & yellow-red jerseys
Long addas on cemented rocks
still rejuvenate me like a sudden
poem in the dingy, smoky coffee house.

Don't look at my face
You may be fooled
Instead dig deep into my heart,
my young heart
I'm waiting for
a magic touch from you
to turn a dry river bed
into a flowing Ganga in search
of the magnanimous ocean

Adda, a Bengali word means informal gossip among friends

Page Mark

The fault was mine, finally
knew when dusk & dust

settled down. Pages thirty two
& thirty three had terrific verse

we always adored in
ecstasy & mud, rains or red

evenings. They turned epistolary
in those rhythmic hours

When dusk & dust settled
& red evenings essayed into

black nights, I discovered yesterday
a forgotten page mark between 32 & 33

Eyes

Consternation is a recent
affair, for scanned
existence
Children ... frolic in the park
Passengers read
favorite books inside long,
white trams
Friends remain surrounding in the
18th century pub

In catatonia however
invisible eyes laugh,
& heart blinks.
Red eyes, or green
prying, piercing through
I try to bleat, but the laughter
gets loud
The pub is erupting this evening ...

In catatonia again, I bleat
for the eyes

Road

Some of you who're already
here (like me), think twice before
any lust, id.
Instead engage in a meta-narrative
of the road, where bumps win
straight lines, where shenanigans
blink wondrous eyes.
If you love the road, lust is all
yours. After all human race must
survive, after all we can't be
sidelined.

But if the road feels craters,
take a break, and think
what loss would the earth incur
if we weren't born,
shenanigans

Amphan 2020

Trees struggled & struggled
to live, they're now
crestfallen, sharing woes
with the road.
The thatched roof of a village
dwelling looks awed from
the top of a surviving dam
Devastated crops are silent,
injured guard to human bodies
A few stray dogs are searching
food, in company of naked
human babies

I'm unable to trudge along
this path of destruction
any more
Lay me beside the crops
I wish to see a clear sky
from my soil
& smiling animals,
again, again & again

(Written a day after the devastating Amphan Cyclone hit
West Bengal, India on 20 May, 2020)

As if I'm

A wry smile only deceives
clever eyes, now & always
Look straight, with shining
eyes; as if I'm the first in the world
to view the morning sun
As if I'm the one with all virtues.
Extend your hand, weak or
robust, which goes deep inside
to unearth all accumulated poems
in mind,
poems that have transcended
coy smile, poems planted in sorrow
and joy, poems to freed me, you

Clever eyes are not permitted
to access a mine of splendid verse.

Good Bye

Let's assume there is a change
Let's assume change always happens
Let's assume all flowers turn into fruits

And all fruits give birth to new saplings.
Only the drain on the roadside laughs
the death of myriad flowers

Let's assume dream changes
every night
But a morbid morning says 'Good Bye'

Birds

Birds, flying in the sky
happy

Or, are they ?
Who knows !
Sky never told you,
me, anybody
Birds never told us

As impending darkness dawns
We birds love to color happiness
& let it survive for the moment, eternally

Dry Ink

Zealous, took up my pen
after decades
& pondered over for hours.
This evening, I wanted to
create something nice
& optimistic, – a poem
of love, or nature, or humanity,
colorful
flowers

Finally when I started
scribbling, found that the ink
had dried long ago

Childish Rains

The taste of needles invading
your already drenched skin is indeed
extraordinary, and the burden
of green mangoes in your
small wet clasps is never a
burden at all.
You get frightened by the
sound and flash of light coming
from above, but that's
full of excitement and revelry.
Green mangoes escaping like
small frogs, and giggling in rain

You're also giggling and
kicking accumulated
water bodies, and your mates
in a never ending show of rains

Tramlines and the Man

Yellow lights were giggling
at the dead of night
There're no buses, trams,
rickshaws or taxis now. All had deserted
the city, sans a lonely man,
possessed by gentle breeze and
glowing lights in a summer night.

Suddenly he heard whispers
He heard whispers ...
Parallel tramlines, happy under the bright lights,
were talking, about their days in the sun,
their ecstasies and agonies.
As history unfolded, the man came to know
about Asia's first tram-city, and
a wonderful metamorphosis from horse driven
tram cars to electric tram cars.

And when the breeze was stronger,
he saw a violent procession approaching tramlines;
and he felt scared initially, but soon realized that
thousands were protesting the partition of their beloved
province.

All of a sudden a big fire appeared and
announced, with pride, the burning of foreign clothes.

Later at night, the man saw a tall figure
with snow white beard
walking along the tramlines.
Look at him, he was also
 the first in Asia to get that coveted prize in literature.
Parallel tramlines raised their heads and bowed down.

Have you seen bright young men running over our bodies
for survival, criss crossing our existence?
But we never felt any pain, as they vowed to build a society
without discrimination, a society we also dreamed.
But we were absolutely pained when an
unmindful poet
fell on us sometimes back

The parallel tramlines were engrossed
in their tales all through the night.
And gradually the man saw another
21st century sun rising slowly
and painting the horizon.
And the whispers had stopped.
All whispers had suddenly stopped...
Silence everywhere.
A deadly Silence
greeted a new dawn
It's the time of uncertainty,
for the tramline and for us.